CRYING IN MY MOTHER'S TONGUE: UKULILA
QHALI

This is a work of fiction. All names, characters, places, and incidents are a product of the author's imagination. Any resemblance to real events or persons, living or dead, is entirely coincidental.

Published by Akashic Books
©2024 Qhali
ISBN: 978-1-63614-215-9

All rights reserved
Printed in China
First printing

Akashic Books
Instagram, X, Facebook: AkashicBooks
info@akashicbooks.com
www.akashicbooks.com

African Poetry Book Fund
Prairie Schooner
University of Nebraska
110 Andrews Hall
Lincoln, Nebraska 68588

Ulwimi: A tongue
Ulwimi: A language
Ulwimi: A lie

***

I live in my mother's tongue
I have had many tongues inside my mouth
Many tongues dying in my mouth
Many tongues growing in my mouth

TABLE OF CONTENTS

Preface by Safia Elhillo 7

daughter 11
January 17, 1994: The Pregnant Tree in Our Village 13
June 1, 1994: Dear Qamata, I need to pray with Makhulu now 14
A Dying 15
Graves 22
June 17, 1994: Dear Qamata, why'd you give tata small hands 23
February 10, 1999: Dear Qamata, did you have a choice? 24
March 19, 2007: Sisi Nokuthula 25

2012—The weight of the years 26
I am a glass 27
the water returns you 29
2013—Three letters I never gave to P 30

August 22, 2014: The prophetess's hand 32
August 1, 2018—Bambo Lwam 33
December 7, 2019: Dear S, I am coming to you 34
August 9, 2020: Dear S, I remember how I came 35
Return to Tsolobeng 36

Acknowledgments 39

PREFACE
by Safia Elhillo

Crying in My Mother's Tongue takes as its central gesture the duality contained in the titular word *tongue*, as language and as organ. These poems embrace the more grotesque aspects of being embodied, one being a mother's tongue and its multiple meanings. Many of the poems contain isiXhosa words, often translated inline in a way that duplicates back on itself, such as in "I am a glass": "Things I licked off *isibeleko sikamama* Things I licked off mama's womb [. . .] *Ingono zam* black monstrous chunks now   My nipples black / monstrous chunks now." The interpretation of *tongue* as language, as Sesotho and isiXhosa, is immediately complicated by the stark physicality of "I have had many tongues inside my mouth," then ventures into the grotesque with "[m]any tongues dying in my mouth" and "[m]any tongues growing in my mouth." Here the unruliness and occasional revulsion that come from being in a body (birth and death, and growth and rot) are expressed. While the tongue is situated in a Sesotho and isiXhosa cultural perspective, it is first and foremost in the body itself, opening it up to a more universal experience of sexual violence and trauma.

    The first poem, "daughter," uses a figurative space—memory and its "corridors"—as a foil for the inescapability of the body, its interruption of even the most cerebral experiences: "big hands pin me down [. . .] where my blood becomes the venom." There is no greater evidence of the indivisibility of mind and body than the fact that smell is one of the great activators of memory. The poet draws on this in the second stanza: "there are smells in the world that freeze me / the past becomes the present."

    In "January 17, 1994: The Pregnant Tree in Our Village," Qhali challenges the binary between the figurative and physical by recounting the myth of a queen with a pregnant tree growing from her back. The pregnant tree can be read as symbol or metaphor, but it's grounded by its literal attachment to the human form. The poem returns often to the word *back*, particularly after fantastical descriptions, like that of the woman covered in yellow snakeskin. This poem also situates the speaker in a Sesotho worldview grounded in the land. If the tree is a woman, a mother, then perhaps the speaker who is both a woman and a mother is also a tree, with roots reaching deep into the ground, which Sesotho people call *home*.

The image of the tongue is wielded to harrowing effect in the poem "A Dying," with its figure of the monster-assailant, whose green tongue "licks the cold off [the speaker's] face" and "licks [the speaker's] eyes open." The line "he is maggots   worming his tongue inside my mouth" alludes to the speaker's silence—the assailant is described as having a tongue, as having a voice, while the speaker has neither. Even in a prolonged description of the speaker's bloodied mouth, the tongue does not appear.

After moving through violence and trauma, the image of the tongue first appears in a declaration of desire in "2013—Three letters I never gave to P": "Dear P, your tongue [. . .] I want to shove you down my throat / to meet you with my tongue." The stanza closes with "I want to follow your tongue / to my father's," making another pairing retrospectively evident: tongue and parent. This pairing invites a closer reading of the title: Mother tongue as first language, but in the case of these poems, as first silence too.

Parental silence is a two-way street in the poem "2012— The weight of years": "She held me / with the quiet between us and I knew that despite the weight of her own story / mine would hurt her more." The speaker's silence in "A Dying" is a result of her protective parental instinct, refusing to wake her daughter and cause her to witness this moment of violence. In "August 22, 2014: The prophetess's hand," an image of the mouth—"a sand of stars / into the mouth of the girl"—leads directly into an image of parenthood—"I swallow / and in the morning I give birth / to a baby girl."

The weight of ancestral reckoning comes to a head in the final two poems. In "August 9, 2020: Dear S, I remember how I came," Qhali reconsiders her relationship to her ancestry—"My first father was Sotho / My last husband was   Suthu"—coming back around with a different understanding of her culture. Likewise in "Return to Tsolobeng," she envisions returning to an ancestral Sesotho community and building a new life there:

> I will wake each day despite the urge to stay on the other side
> to build a home in Tsolobeng
> so I teach my children what is in a name
> so a life of color is not that of complexion
> so a life of wealth is not that of the tangibles
> so that each click that comes out of my mouth
> has a root with a home they can call their own

Such is the deft weave-work of Qhali's *Crying in My Mother's Tongue*. It's an intricate tapestry in which language braids to the body, disappearing for a time into silence during its violation, emerging anew to demand witness, to brazenly detail every image of the grotesque, and finally to return to the land. Silence is woven to the parental figure in moments without access to Sesotho language and culture, which are inherited from her distant parents but not fully passed down, and in moments when silence is an act of care, of protection, from parent to child or from child to parent. And throughout, the body's faculties, its bluntly named and gleefully described parts, are a portal into memory, smells jostling awake the mind.

DAUGHTER

there are corridors in my memory
i shall now take you into
dark rooms in which i am blind and see everything
where big hands pin me down
feasting on me   dead   breathing
where my blood becomes the venom
where no one saves me

there are smells in the world that freeze me
the past becomes the present   keeps me from leaving
where a moonlike taste
and purple futures are still waiting

i was born with the storm inside me
at the center is the dark and the light
it is the dark that held me longest

and this
is the story of day and night
of home
of no place of beauty and of love

eli libali lomfazi   this is the story of a woman
moving between time
between worlds
reaching for her mother
outside her waters
eli libali lomzimba   this is the story of a body
dying

and being born
on the edge of something dreamed of

this is the story of a girl
and i loved her
i loved her

JANUARY 17, 1994: THE PREGNANT TREE IN OUR VILLAGE

In a village called Tsolobeng over the Tina river
there is an empty house built upon the bones of a queen
   Mamorena   they called her
She birthed six kings   one died on her back
three months old   and where he died
a pregnant tree pushed out
right from the center of her back
Hunched like this she walked
a tall Sesotho creature   Mamorena
covered in yellow snake's skin
with a towering brown tree on her back
Since her mate disappeared into the ground
they say the men in her village dared not to look into her blue eyes
They all heard of the one who drowned in her
But I did   I grew up going into her
never wanting to come out

JUNE 1, 1994: DEAR QAMATA, I NEED TO PRAY WITH MAKHULU NOW

there is too much moving around in this house   bags being packed and unpacked   broken glass on the floor then in mama's hands   loud screaming in my ears   then whispering women in my sleep   and no praying   the other day i got dropped off at Makhulu's   and very few many days later i got taken away from her   i didn't want to leave her   but no one ever asks me what i want   and tata says children must keep quiet when big people talk   so i keep quiet all the time   but i try this thing where i tell them with my eyes   sometimes i see them look and all the time i see them hear   but they say nothing   i didn't mind not playing with my friends at my school   Makhulu's school   at home   was so much better   she said at hers when i open my eyes we start   i didn't mind being cold once a day watching water cook on a fire that she made so i could bath   i didn't mind eating only isidudu every day for breakfast then chasing a chicken that scared me for dinner   watching other children play while they waited for me to finish making bread with my fists   having to sit on the floor   and wait my turn in a circle with one plate and seven other children to eat lunch with my fingers   climbing her trees to look for ripe peaches and hiding in my mouth the greens ones   filling her bucket with apricots then walking all alone to her neighbour to trade them for mealies   i didn't mind being sent up the hill twice a day for i-stoney and being chased down the hill by a brown dog so i couldn't steal any of it   all the way home   i didn't mind falling and cutting my knee open   and Makhulu blowing the blood back into me then telling me to go play the pain away   washing in a little red vas'kom where i couldn't stretch my legs but had to make sure i washed away all the day and all the night before i went into   new ones   singing over words that i couldn't understand every night for an hour from a hymn book written in my mother's tongue to earn my sleep   i didn't mind falling asleep listening to her pray for me and my teachers   and my mama and my sisi   and my mama's sisters and all her children   and her children's children and my tata   and my tata's mother and her children   and her mama and her tata   and their mothers   and their fathers   and her church   and her friends and her neighbors   and her mamazala and her sisters from her mamazala   and their brothers and for her husband and everyone with him to take all her prayers to you Qamata

A DYING

Sssssh   he says

His green tongue licks the cold off my face

You fucking make a sound and this knife will fuck you before I do

I do as he says
Not because of the knife walking my throat
My daughter is sleeping in her bedroom   less than 6 steps

I can hear her breathing
I plead silently   God   deafen this monster so he doesn't hear my girl

I hear her
Her chest moving up and down
My eyes shut
Her breath dancing in and out
I focus on this
I focus on her
For a moment I can forget the face on top of me
For a moment I am not in this moment

He licks my eyes open   He whispers

God is quiet
The man is pushing me into my bed
I don't fight him
I cannot fight   him   My daughter
I want to sink

I want to drown   but the mattress   It's fighting him

A small cry slips out   I have been crying for a while
Saliva down my mouth   This is real
He is real

This is fear

I want to fight back   my daughter's face tells me not to
She is inside my eyes
He bends   his heavy long upper body   over my small frame

He comes back up with a red brick
My eyes open   I recognize the brick:
I have a pile of bricks outside
I was going to finish building the wall

It's my fault   This nightmare is my fault

How did he get inside my house   without me hearing?
He had to break something
Did I not lock the sliding door?
No   I did   I did?
Does he have a key?
Does this person know me?
The brick   Why is he holding a brick above my face?
Is he going to kill me?
If he wants to kill me—he has a knife
Why is he not stabbing me?
Why is he holding a brick above me?

He answers
A kettle boiling in my ears
Loud
Hot

This is pain

It is dark
He comes back at me again with the brick
I'm out   I'm in   I'm out
Blood is lava in my mouth
A thick oozing in between my teeth
I am choking on my blood
I can't cough   But I do   A little
I will wake her up
So I swallow

Blood is running down my face
Blood is pouring
I want to cough

This is panic

He puts the brick down on the empty side of the bed   Gently
He is delicate with it
Settles it down beside me   a lover   for later
I am out   I am in

God   please save me

The man on top of me grunting pulls his penis out of his pants
A breathing snake falls onto my stomach
God is quiet
He hits me with it   His penis
I want to ask him to take everything
Everything I no longer care about
But I don't move
I don't speak
God is quiet

This is helplessness

He picks up the knife   from beside the brick
He slides the blade down my neck   his legs
straddled across me
I didn't realize how close it was
I could have killed him   Maybe

The snake is getting stronger
Has been waiting
on my stomach
The snake is moving on top of me
A hard snake is on top of me

The knife moves up and down my ribs
I think the knife cums   I'm not sure
The knife smiles   Tries to cut my gown
My gown fights back

Qamata

My stupid gown makes him mad
I beg my gown not to provoke him
Please   I'm sorry
He thinks I am talking to him
This makes him hard on top of my stomach   again

This is darkness

I am not afraid of the knife
I am not afraid of dying
I am afraid of waking my daughter
I am afraid she will know I am in the danger
the way she knows when I need a hug
I am afraid of leaving my child   in this place
I need to lie still now

This is fear

He is maggots   worming his tongue inside my mouth
Soiling my bed
My stink mixed with his stink

Shit   and urine   mix   move   slowly under me
move slowly towards him
He feels it all

I am angry at myself
I know what is coming
a thousand bricks on my head
Crashing bricks inside my head

I don't move

A burning ocean inside me

I don't move

This is fire

This man wants me dead
An angry brick against my head
My daughter   A brick breaks against me
Qamata   where are you?   I am all she has

My daughter   I can hear her voice
I can hear her
What is she doing?
Wake up mama!
She is not here
I am alone   No one will save me

I am sorry bhuti

He smiles with his yellow teeth
I can smell the plaque and blood and death in his mouth
My eyes are crying
crying will not save us
He stretches my legs as far apart as they will allow
I concede
He pushes inside me
Penis   in my lungs
Penis   in my fingertips

This is dying

GRAVES

Abanye abafazi ngamangcwaba
agrunjwa ngoyise abangabaziyo
abanye otata bagrumba nzulu
kumhlaba ongadalelwangwa bona

AMANGCWABA

Other women are graves
dug by fathers they have never met
others by fathers who dug too deep
into places they should never go

JUNE 17, 1994: DEAR QAMATA, WHY'D YOU GIVE TATA SMALL HANDS

tata's hands are too small
to hold umama
so he cuts her up to make her fit
he cannot have *umfazi*[1] bigger than him
living in his house

every night
tata dilutes his blood *nomchamo wabelungu*[2]
i guess it tastes better than his own
he's trying to quiet the dead ones in him
but the smell of death won't leave his bones

mama's bones cry to put tata to sleep
but only her blood pouring
let's him know he's won
i'm not allowed to swim in mama's blood anymore

but i am allowed to watch her clean it up
allowed to help her pull him up
allowed to wash *ibhakethi elimbomvu*[3]
after she offers *igazi lakhe*[4] to the soil

i am never alone   the moon became my friend
and only other witness of how umama plays dead
then trades her blood *nabangaphantsi*[5]
for more time

---

1 umfazi   a woman
2 nomchamo wabelungu   with white man's urine
3 ibhaketi elimbomvu   a red bucket
4 igazi lakhe   their blood
5 nabangaphantsi   with the ones below

FEBRUARY 10, 1999: DEAR QAMATA, DID YOU HAVE A CHOICE?

i think they lied about you in the bible   i think they lied about esther eve and
    mary too
but the biggest lie was god being you   i don't think you have a penis   what purpose
would that serve   in what eternal place would a creator actually choose to be male
i guess if you were here on earth that would make sense   but on the other side
in heaven   i don't know   Jesus may have been a man here   but chances are
if he cried out that day it was *Mother, Mother,* who would forgive

MARCH 19, 2007: SISI NOKUTHULA

Do you remember how you called me sisi
but i was only one year ahead of you?

I spent one-hundred-and-fifty days
counting scars to see your face

You taught me how to
listen to Notomato's tales of her parents

to forget about my own
How to make black ice cream with Kool-Aid and a ShopRite plastic

We would smile   each smile teaching the other
the new languages we had to learn

You taught me
how to jump over torn pantyhose

Quietly land on the other side
Smile

You said I had been here before
I felt   the same about you

2012—THE WEIGHT OF THE YEARS

My sister fished me out of the water last year   She took me to umama and begged her to save me   I think she didn't know that you don't bring a woman a child that she cannot save and expect her to stay the same   Tata knew the weight of a calling and failing   That's why he got into his car and left town   Mama knew the limits of her body   She didn't say a word   She only tried to hold me   but my breath was too heavy   She lay beside me   I felt I could drown in her waters but I saw lungs die inside her   She held me with the quiet between us and I knew that despite the weight of her own story mine would hurt her more

I AM A GLASS

I am a glass
I don't break
I don't burn
I am fighting flames off my skin
Ulwimi lwam luyatsha   My tongue is burning
Ilizwi liyatsha   My voice is burning
Aniboni? Ndiyatsha!   Can you not see? I am burning!
Things that once lived in me
are dead
Things I licked off *isibeleko sikamama*   Things I licked off mama's womb

And there is a lump
growing
inside me
beating

It is made of her blood
so it grows

It should not be growing
but it is her

This black body
holding it
is burning
I am black
I am burning
I am red
I am burning

I am a scab

Ingono zam black monstrous chunks now   My nipples
Intliziyo yam   My heart
ibetha emaqatheni   beat at my ankles

All stuck in this bottle with me
All charred pieces of flesh for the animal's now
And I am stuck in this bottle
And he is out there

Smiling

To have gotten away with it

To have gotten away with it

THE WATER RETURNS YOU

i found it above me on a tree and asked it why They didn't take me when i went in it got up and flew away   i followed it   umama told the psychiatrist i was in the garden   suddenly got up   started laughing   looked at the sun started crying   and i fell down   what i wanted to tell the psychiatrist: *i was once happy and perhaps someday i will be   but that day the earth swallowed me i woke up sleeping on red soil   when i rose i followed a black bird   it led me to a village of old women with red clay on their faces floating above the soil   alone in the center of that familiar place with* iingwevukazi *floating above me was a big black rock   the bird perched on it and it woke up   the rock told me to return to this place   to the land of the walking   told me that someone i had left the waters with was waiting for me   that i would hear Them call my name when i was ready*

2013—THREE LETTERS I NEVER GAVE TO P

I.   Dear P, your tongue

I want you in my mouth
I want your face inside my mouth
I want to shove you down my throat
to meet you with my tongue
I don't want you to speak outside me
I want to swallow you
I want to follow your tongue
to my father's

II.   Dear P, to lay with you

When you climb my bones eyes closed you tear into me blindly   into a womb trembling you dig deeper to feel the wound I cannot see   bleeding   beneath your waist my spirit is a violent storm as the wound grows   can you really not feel it or do you simply enjoy me dying?

III.   Dear P, don't wake me up

You wake me up at night in your bed sweating   annoyed that i am pouring water   you do not know the damage you do: i am a whale swimming alone   inside   these waters i hear a song   faint   but i know it i swim towards the song   when i almost reach the faces of the song i hear a child crying   on the shore i know it is my child   i am swimming towards the child   in my belly when i reach the shore and lift my head   you wake me up

AUGUST 22, 2014: THE PROPHETESS'S HAND

Back against the bed
                a hand rises
tears through the roof
breaking into the sky
it gathers a handful of stars

Comes back down *inkosazana*   a princess
Leaving behind *iinkosi*   old kings

In silence they watch
the prophetesses hand
planting *iinkwenkwenzi*   a sand of stars
into the mouth of the girl

I swallow
and in the morning I give birth
to a baby girl

AUGUST 1, 2018—BAMBO LWAM

You
found me
in the forest
naked
trembling
an animal
wounded
lost
no home
losing
from a heart
turned cold

You
undressed
your skin
surrendered
to the soil
to lie
beside me
my fire

I woke up
alive
to you
sleeping

DECEMBER 7, 2019: DEAR S, I AM COMING TO YOU

My last night on your chest your thin black hairs folded
as I came down   They made a fire for my bones
Your ribs softened enough for my spine to feel sheltered
And I did   I did

And then the morning came   tearing
stretching   determined   unsoftened by a life
that would not tear

You reasoned for another ending
Pleading   to an unrelenting Hand

Now   I hear you calling me everywhere
In the sea I hear my name   It is not this one
But I know it is mine   I want to go in
I hear you calling me in crowds   I want to go in
Driving on the N2 back home I hear you
In the rocks along the road I want to stop the car   I want to go in
But I am not alone   The trees behind them move
I am not alone   I hear you   I want to call back to you

Collect me on the edge where they took you
Bring me stories of Nkgono Makhulu Nokuthula and everyone
You will tell me your tales in your new language on our way back home
I have so much to teach you too

AUGUST 9, 2020: DEAR S, I REMEMBER HOW I CAME

My first father was   Sotho
My last husband was   Suthu
They once were one
I lost my first father before I came here
I left him with my 7th father's seed
This is how to make love to make me
Suthu I see   .
It is heavy to cross over but this is how

In the darkness your hand always found mine
To keep me from going too deep into the water
You knew better how to walk under water
What to take and what to bring them
to let you come back to me
They took you long before your body stopped
And we were only granted enough time
to help me return to you one day

RETURN TO TSOLOBENG

Two cubs in my hands
one with open eyes—the other asleep
I'm placing them in my mother's palms
tougher than mine—to shield them
I'm going to the mountains for a while
where two old women wait for me
outside a green hut guarded by brown horses
at the top of a hidden mountain
overlooking an old river full of queens and secrets
The two old women will only watch me as I build
with hands covered in manure to cast walls to find me
and I will sleep only to visit the elders but I will wake
with the ones that do not speak to save my children
from a life without rivers and mountains and horses
and quiet and land and snow and a mother
I will wake each day despite the urge to stay on the other side
to build a home in Tsolobeng
so I teach my children what is in a name
so a life of color is not that of complexion
so a life of wealth is not that of the tangibles
so that each click that comes out of my mouth
has a root with a home they can call their own
I have been missing for a while   long before this trip
Sometimes a mother needs to return home to be a mother
because sometimes this place can make you forget
how to be a human
how to feed a child and be nowhere else
how to look at a child with open eyes
which turns you took that cut wires in you

because you are on an edge and the mind is screaming
and they are screaming and the world is screaming
and if you say one more word or take one more wrong turn
whatever colorful string is holding your body together with your soul
will unravel
I am going back to Tsolobeng
back to my ancestors' land
where truth and sanity
wait in whispers

ACKNOWLEDGMENTS

The poem "June 17, 1994: Dear Qamata, why'd you give tata small hands" was first published in *Kalahari Review;* "Return to Tsolobeng" was first published in *Red Wheelbarrow.*